Contents

Gillian Cross (b.1945) is one of the world's leading children's writers.

She has written over 30 books for children, including *Wolf*, which won the

Carnegie Medal, and *The Great Elephant Chase*, which won the Smarties

Grand Prix and the Whitbread Award. She lives in Warwickshire with

her husband; they have four children.

An interview with
Gillian Cross
by Julia Eccleshare

My family

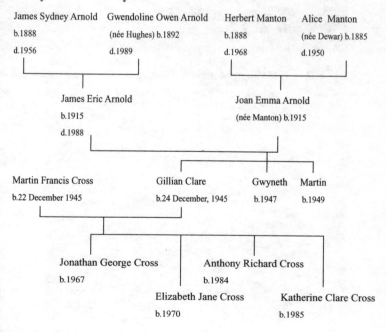

James Sydney Arnold
b.1888
d.1956

Gwendoline Owen Arnold
(née Hughes) b.1892
d.1989

Herbert Manton
b.1888
d.1968

Alice Manton
(née Dewar) b.1885
d.1950

James Eric Arnold
b.1915
d.1988

Joan Emma Arnold
(née Manton) b.1915

Martin Francis Cross
b.22 December 1945

Gillian Clare
b.24 December, 1945

Gwyneth
b.1947

Martin
b.1949

Jonathan George Cross
b.1967

Anthony Richard Cross
b.1984

Elizabeth Jane Cross
b.1970

Katherine Clare Cross
b.1985

Did your grandparents play any part in your family life?

My father's father worked in the Central Telegraph Office in London and died when I was quite young, but my grandmother on that side lived until she was 97. She lived fairly close when I was a child (although she lived in Africa later on) and she was around quite a lot.

Gillian's great-grandfather, Joseph Manton (right), on his engine.

My mother's mother died when I was about five. She had been the Captain of the Furnivall Sculling Club, and sculled in its Ladies' Eight (in a dress with leg o'mutton sleeves, I believe). My mother's father lived to be 80 and we saw quite a lot of him, too.

My great-grandfather on my mother's side lived to be about 95 and I remember him well. He came from Lincolnshire and worked on the railways. He used to read Dickens' books over and over again.

My grandfather on that side was in the Grenadier Guards in World War I and then worked as a commercial traveller for Fry's.

What did your parents do?

My mother was a teacher. She taught English and French and was a great influence on me. My father had a chemistry degree and a PhD and he worked in the paint industry,

Gillian's father, James Eric Arnold, with Pharaoh, his eagle owl.

but music was his great passion. He was organist and choirmaster at All Saints', Margaret Street in London

(a church which is famous for its music). My grandmother and aunt used to go there too, but it was rather a
long journey, so the rest of us went to the local church in
Harrow-on- the-Hill. My father had a pet eagle owl
called Pharaoh.

Who did you get on with best?

I was quite solitary in the family, but quite sociable at
school. I read a lot of the time when I was at home.

What animals, if any, were part of the household?

We had two cats, Kitty and Johnny. Kitty was an old
black cat who stayed inside. Johnny was a younger
tabby and white cat who stayed outside. My sister
had guinea pigs and a hamster, but I've never wanted
to own animals. I'm not a very animally kind
of person.

My childhood

Where were you born?

I was born in Fairlight Nursing Home, Woodside Park,
London N12.

What was your house like?

When I was six we moved to 19 Greystone Gardens, Kenton, in Harrow. It was a detached, red brick house with five bedrooms. It was in a long, long garden – one third of an acre. It had once had a tennis court and there was a small orchard. When we moved in, it was very overgrown and I remember it as a wilderness. Later on, it became a lovely garden. I liked the house and the garden.

Gillian and her brother and sister in the garden of
19 Greystone Gardens (1952 approx).

What was the nearest town and what did you like about it?

Kenton is a post-war suburb. My mother can remember it as farmland, but by my childhood it had been built over. I never had much sense of place when I was a child and I'm sure that is because I lived in a suburb. It was very featureless and shapeless and I was quite far away from my friends. It was only when I went to Oxford that I began to develop a sense of place.

Was your childhood happy?

Oh yes. I think of it as very happy, but I can't remember the details very clearly. I know that I read a lot and that I was happy in the garden.

What is your best memory of it?

I have lots of nice memories. I used to like wandering around the garden just poking about. The garden is a big factor in my childhood memories.

What is your worst memory of it?

My worst memory of my childhood is that my mother

had a locket and I stole it and hid it in the doll's house. It was dreadful!

Gillian (right) with her sister, Gwyneth and brother, Martin.

What frightened you or made you sad?

I don't think that anything made me sad. But I did sometimes get frightened. One time, having read

7

about people climbing out of windows with a sheet, I decided to try it. I gave the end to one of my siblings to hold. Luckily my mother arrived in the nick of time!

My schooldays

What was your first school like?

It was called Preston Park School. I can remember the communal violin lessons. We were too young to join in, so we just watched. I then went to Mount Stewart, a big new primary school for 6–11 year-olds.

When did you learn to read?

I learned to read at school on Janet and John books. I didn't find it hard.

What was your secondary school like?

It was great; as a place it was lovely. North London Collegiate School is built in a huge park. There is an old house at the centre of the school with some new building around it. North London allowed me to be what I needed to be. It also made you think about other people. Dame Kitty Anderson, the head-mistress, was keen that we were aware of children who were less lucky than we were. When we were applying to university she pointed out that some children our age were paying taxes which would pay for our university fees. I'm still in touch with a lot of people from school. I made good friends there.

**Gillian in her
North London Collegiate
School uniform (1957).**

What was your favourite subject?

Mostly English, and history, too. And I liked maths.

What was your most hated subject?

Geography.

Who was your favourite teacher?

There were a lot of teachers whom I was fond of. The English teacher, Miss Clay would argue with us and I really liked that. She was in charge of the school magazine and I edited it. I got to do that because I wasn't elected to be a prefect. I was a bit miffed about that at the time.

What was your worst subject?

Geography.

What subject did you do best?

English.

What was your handwriting like then?

Dreadful! I had to sit at the front of the class because it was so bad. They taught us all italic, but I couldn't do it.

Did any teacher think you might become a writer?

If they did, they didn't tell me!

What did reading mean to you?

Reading was a thing that I did automatically. It was very important for me to have private reading. It was important for me not to share those sorts of things. If you haven't got enormous confidence, it's important that you build it up. You have to bounce off your own responses.

What did words mean to you?

I used to keep a little book and write down words I liked.

What is it now?

Alan Bennett's *Talking Heads*.

My career

What did you do when you left school?

My further education was at Somerville College, Oxford where I read English. I then went to Sussex University and got a further degree (a DPhil).

What was your first job?

I've never had a full-time job. I've worked part-time in the office of the Labour MP for Gravesend, I've worked in a village bakery and I've been a Community Service Volunteer, working as an untrained teacher and as a residential worker for teenagers with special educational needs. I have also been a school governor and chairperson of the PTA.

I have four children, the first of whom was born when I was at Oxford, so my jobs have always fitted around being at home and writing.

My children have filled a lot of the space that might have been given to a job. Keeping in touch with them, their friends and their schools have often given me good background information for my books. I never use my own children as models for my stories but I used to tell stories to them sometimes.

My career as a writer

Did you write as a child – poetry, stories, plays?

I wrote the beginnings of things. Mostly stories, but once I wrote a play with friends at school. When I was a teenager I wrote poetry.

When did you decide to become a professional writer?

Never. It just happened.

How did you start to write?

There were three triggers.

First, I was a founder member of the Lewes Children's Book Group where I met lots of people who read children's books.

The second was that I read *The Beethoven Medal* by K.M. Peyton all in one go and I thought it was fantastic. I wrote to K.M. Peyton and she wrote a lovely letter back. It was my first contact with a writer.

The third was that in around 1974 I said to Nicholas Tucker, who taught at Sussex University, 'Everything I write sounds so dreadful.' He said, 'Of course it does to you.' Those three things inspired me, so I bought some ear plugs and wrote a book which no one published, but it got me into writing.

Who encouraged you?

My husband Martin Cross was very encouraging. He still reads everything I write and often helps with titles. Nicholas Tucker was also very helpful.

Who inspired you?

Peter Dickinson and K.M. Peyton.

What do you like best about writing?

I like the fact that I can be exactly what I like on my own. I like the fact that it stretches me as a person.

What, if anything, do you hate about it?

I don't hate anything. I like it all.

Is writing an obsession or compulsion?

Less so than it used to be.

Is it a lonely profession?

It's solitary, not lonely.

Do you find writing hard?

Yes, it is hard and I work hard at it.

Did you start with habits that you've changed?

Yes. I used to write in long-hand and then type. Now I work on a computer.

How long does it take you to write a book?

It depends what kind of book it is. I write for different ages. Some are very quick; others take a lot of research before I can get going.

Do you rewrite?

Yes, lots.

Do you let anyone read your manuscript before it is finished?

I don't let anyone read it before it is finished but I'm desperate for someone to read it as soon as it is finished. My husband Martin reads everything I've written and Katy and Anthony sometimes do.

Do you listen to criticism?

Yes, from everybody. I like revising. I almost always revise it after my editor sees it.

Why do you write for children?

I like writing for children because the story is allowed to be the most important thing. I like action, what people do, not what they are like.

What subjects appeal to you?

I like to write about different subjects all the time.

What kind of research do you do?

Whatever is necessary for the particular book – reading, visits. For *Wolf* I went to London Zoo so that I could

study the wolves. I was invited to go into the cage.
It's about the only real thing I've ever used in a book.
It crystallised what I thought.

I visit places where I set books – but not abroad. For
The Great Elephant Chase I got stacks of stuff from the
US historical societies – far more than I needed – but it
provided very useful background information. I also talk to
people to find things out. I ask all kinds of nosy questions.
Schools provide a lot of useful background information as
well. I've always had a lot of contact with schools.

How important is imagination?
It is the most important thing. It is central to any book.

Do you base your situations on real life?
No.

Do you base your characters on real people?
No.

What matters most to you, the story or the characters?
The story, but you can't disentangle them.

Who do you write for?

If I think about it at all, a not very bookish 13-year-old boy who will be easily bored. Mostly, I do what I like.

Which of your own books is your favourite and who is your favourite character?

I haven't got one favourite book, but I could choose a few. *Wolf*, *The Great Elephant Chase*, *The Tree House* and *Chartbreak* are all titles that I like a lot.

My favourite character is Clipper in *Save Our School*. I like pretending to be her. Also, Finch in *Chartbreak*.

Are pictures important in your books?

Yes, in some. In *Beware Olga!* I love the picture of Olga screaming.

What gives you most satisfaction about being a writer?

The bit when you've been in a terrible muddle and you suddenly see how it has to be. I've never started a book without knowing the beginning. I know what sort of end it will be, but not exactly what it is.

What do you hope to achieve with your books?

I hope to write stories that people will like to read. I don't aim to manipulate the reader at all.

Why are books important?

Books are important because they open up knowledge, experience, everything. They make lots of things possible which you couldn't actually act out. They offer such a lot of variety. They can operate with small audiences – unlike TV.

Why is fiction important?
Will it still be important in the new century?

We don't know why fiction is important, but we know that it is. Yes, of course it will be important in the new century. Especially because we don't know why.

Do you think that TV can complement reading or be a substitute for it?

TV can complement reading. For some people it is how they get their fiction. It doesn't stop people reading.

Which book, either children's or adult, has influenced your life?

The Bible and Shakespeare.

What book comforts you most?

The same!

My top ten favourite books (more or less) when I was a child and why I have chosen them.

1. *The Secret Garden* by Frances Hodgson Burnett

This has always been my favourite book.

2. *Swallows and Amazons* by Arthur Ransome

I enjoyed books about camping and surviving in the open air, and this book and its sequels are wonderful outdoor adventures.

3. *The Magic Faraway Tree* by Enid Blyton

I'd like to say that I enjoyed it because of the wonderful countries at the top of the tree. But I think the wonderful food and the Slippery-Slip had more to do with it.

4. *What Katy Did at School* by Susan Coolidge

I liked *What Katy Did* as well, but I preferred this one, because of the games they play at school – and the wonderful parcel they get from home.

5. *Little Women* by Louisa May Alcott

I must have read this dozens of times. I especially liked the newspaper the girls wrote.

6. *National Velvet* by Enid Bagnold

I thought this was the best horse book ever – and I still do.

7. The complete catalogue of plays published by Samuel French Ltd. It didn't look very exciting, but it was like reading hundreds of stories, all compressed into two or three lines.

8. *The Little Grey Men* by B.B.

This is a story about gnomes, but they're not whimsical. I loved the realistic details of their lives beside the stream.

9. *Ballet Shoes* by Noel Streatfeild

I wasn't good at ballet, but I desperately wanted to be an actress, so Pauline was my favourite character in the book.

10. *The Swish of the Curtain* by Pamela Brown

This is about a group of children who form a theatre company. I adored it, and I wanted to be them.

Ten of my favourites from the books for children that I have read since I was a grown up.

1. *Tulku* by Peter Dickinson

I've mentioned this before.

2. *The Three Royal Monkeys* by Walter de la Mare

This is a strange and magical book, like nothing else.

3. *The Beethoven Medal* by K.M. Peyton

This is the book that really started me off as a writer. It's about love and music.

4. *Falling into Glory* by Robert Westall

This one's about love and rugby. A serious book.

5. *The Other Side of Silence* by Margaret Mahy
I think that Margaret Mahy is an amazing writer and this is one of her best books.

6. *Coming to Tea* by Sarah Garland
This is a picture book, and children probably think it's for them. But it's the best book I know about what it's really like to be a mother with small children.

7. *Katie Morag and the Tiresome Ted*
by Mairi Hedderwick
I love all Mairi Hedderwick's beautiful picture books about Katie Morag and her lovely Scottish island.

8. *The Owl Service* by Alan Garner
This is mysterious, mythological and modern.

9. *A Swarm in May* by William Mayne
William Mayne is one of my favourite writers and I like all his books, but I have an especially soft spot for this one.

10. *The Exiles at Home* by Hilary Mackay

This is funny and serious and full of good things. A very satisfying book.

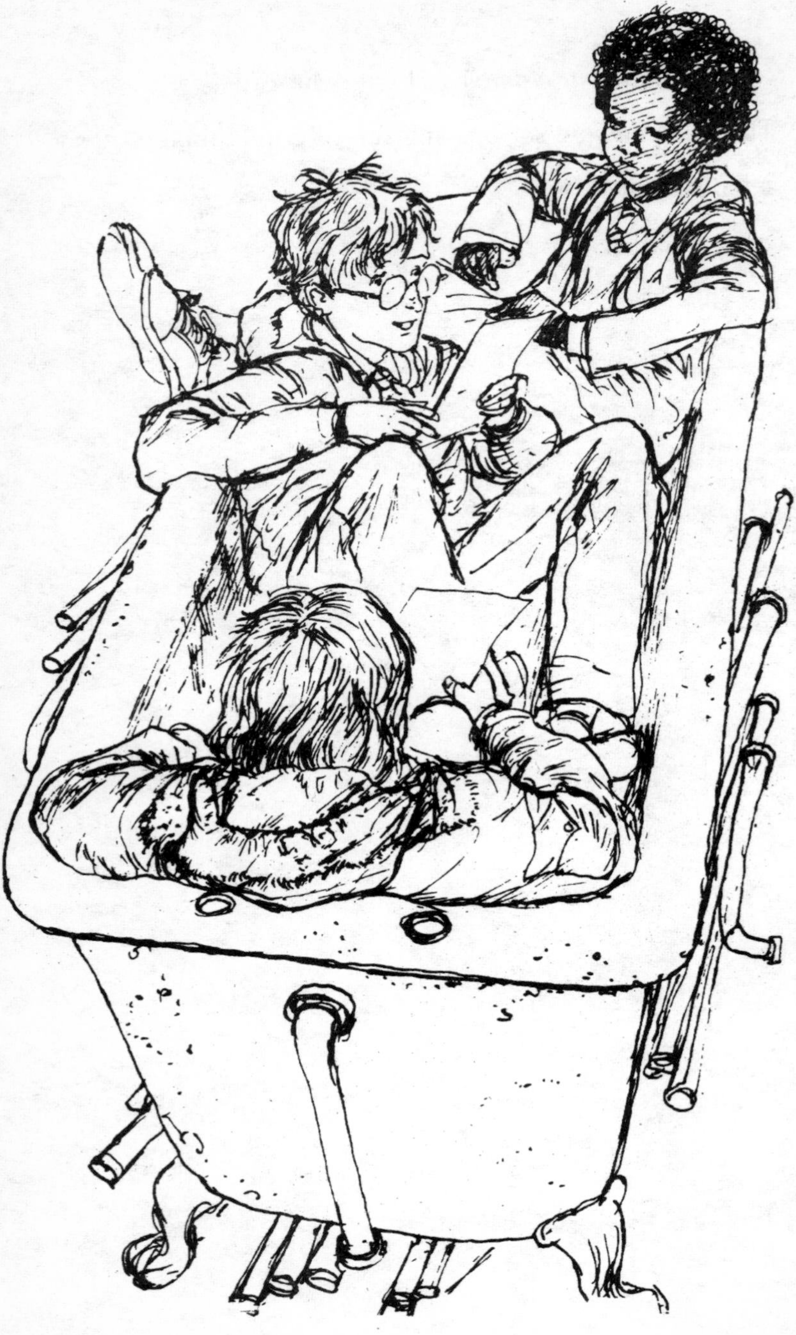

Illustration by Gareth Floyd for *Save Our School*

Gillian's Books
An overview by Julia Eccleshare

GILLIAN CROSS is one of the most popular and successful writers of today. Her first book was published in 1979 and since then she has written over thirty books – quite an achievement in twenty years! Her books have been recorded on tape, adapted for TV and turned into plays. She has also won all the major book prizes. *Wolf* was published in 1990 and won the Carnegie Medal while *The Great Elephant Chase*, published in 1992, won the Smarties Prize and the Whitbread Children's Book Prize.

Wolf

The Great Elephant Chase

But it is not only for those books that Gillian is such a popular writer. All of her books have an immediate appeal for readers of all ages. She is not a writer whom it is easy to pigeonhole, because with almost every book she embarks on something new. Because of this, her books are always interesting and often surprising. It also means that her writing has an enthusiastic feeling, as if she is enjoying telling the story as much as you are enjoying reading it.

Inspiration

The Demon Headmaster series

The only time she has come near to repeating herself is with *The Revenge of the Demon Headmaster*, *The Demon Headmaster Strikes Again* and *The Demon Headmaster Takes Over*, the sequels to *The Demon Headmaster* which inevitably use the same characters and the same setting. Those apart, all sorts of things may trigger a story for her to tell. Sometimes it's a place, sometimes it's an event and sometimes it's the voice of one of the characters.

Roscoe's Leap

Roscoe's Leap is the best example of a story of Gillian's that was inspired by a visit to a place. *Roscoe's Leap* is set in an extraordinary house, which has been built in two parts joined together by a bridge over a thundering stream. The idea for the house came from a visit Gillian made to Cragside, a stately home in Northumberland which was the first private house in Britain to have electricity. It, too, is an extraordinary house and the huge and complicated turbines which powered the electricity are an important part of it.

It was the voice that Gillian had first when she started to write *Chartbreak*, a story about a girl singer in a pop group. In fact, she had the voice of the girl, who became Finch, in her head for some time before she knew exactly what the story would be.

Chartbreak

Though the inspirations and ideas for Gillian's stories come from a variety of sources there is a thread that links all of her books. They are all adventures with a lot of action and a well-constructed plot. Once you've started reading one of Gillian's books, whether it's for older readers like *A Map of Nowhere*, or one of her books for young readers like *Beware Olga!*, you can't put it down. She always makes you want to find out what happens next.

A Map of Nowhere

Beware Olga!

Past and present

Gillian writes comfortably about the past and the present, and has set her stories in both. In 1979 she had her first two books published. One was historical and one was set in the present. Since then, she has written more books of both kinds though nowadays she writes more that are contemporary, reflecting the lives of her readers.

Her first historical book, *The Iron Way* was about the building of the railways in Victorian England. Others with historical backgrounds are *A Whisper of Lace*, which is about lace smuggling in the eighteenth century, and *The Great Elephant Chase*, which is set in America at the end of the nineteenth century. In all of these,

The Iron Way

A Whisper of Lace

The Great Elephant Chase

Gillian brings the past to life convincingly so that it feels interestingly different but the people react in recognisable and familiar ways.

The way the past affects the present is a theme that she uses in several of her books. In *Roscoe's Leap* an unhappy family past needs to be laid to rest before the present-day children, Stephen and Hannah, can be happy, and in *The Dark Behind the Curtain* a school production of *Sweeney Todd* summons up ghostly, frightened children from Victorian times. In these books Gillian makes readers aware of how important history is and how the past needs to be respected and understood.

Roscoe's Leap

The Dark Behind the Curtain

Gillian's first contemporary story, *The Runaway*, was published in 1979, the same year as *The Iron Way*, and has many of the characteristics of her later books. Denny runs away after his granny's accident rather than having to go and stay in the council children's home. He meets up with Nachtar who happens to be play-

The Runaway

ing truant that day and together they find food for Denny and a place for him to stay. Managing without being discovered by the grown-ups, especially by Nachtar's strict father, is hard and in the end adults are needed to reunite Denny and his grandmother. Gillian's description of the boys' lives is very accurate for the time (and quite dated now!).

Many of Gillian's books for younger readers have the same kinds of ingredients. They are about modern children coping on their own and they are set in very familiar schools and streets — the kinds of places where adventures really do take place.

Story

Whatever the background, historical or contemporary, Gillian writes to entertain her readers and to keep them fully absorbed in the twists and turns of the story.

It is this ability to tell a good story that

makes all of Gillian's books so exciting and so readable. There is always an element of danger or fear. Sometimes she uses really frightening settings and situations, such as the kidnapping storyline in *On the Edge* in which Tug, the son of a famous journalist, has to survive both physical and mental pressure when he is taken hostage. Or in *Wolf*, which also has a frightening background of explosives and terrorism against which Cassie's story is told.

On the Edge

Wolf

More commonly, there is nothing particularly frightening about the setting but there is a lot of tension in the plot. This is especially true in the Clipper, Spag and Barny stories such as *Save Our School*, *Swimathon!* and *The Mintyglo Kid*. Everything about the background to these books is familiar but Gillian has a remarkable gift for describing the incredible tension of the situations in which the children find themselves. In *Swimathon!* the chances of the gang winning the swimming competition look very slight

Save Our School

Swimathon!

The Mintyglo Kid

indeed when Spag and Barny discover that Clipper can't even swim. Right up until the nail-biting finish their money and reputation look like being at stake. Gillian keeps up the excitement and the suspense and then finds a very neat way of resolving it. Similarly, in *Rescuing Gloria*, Leo gets into more and more predicaments from the first ridiculous moment when he pushes the goat home in a pram, hoping that no one will look too closely. Keeping the goat, and then the ducks, hens and other strays a secret doesn't have any danger about it but, nonetheless, there is a spicy element of excitement as he and his friends try to cope without adult help.

Rescuing Gloria

Whatever the drama, whether genuinely life-threatening or merely risky, Gillian conveys the mood so well that everyone shares the fears of the children who are at the heart of them. She always presents dangerous and difficult situations for her characters to handle which, when resolved, never give the impression that there was an unlikely or easy way out. The endings are always as satisfying as the beginnings and the cliff-hangers along the way keep the stories going.

Gillian believes that a good story is vital to keep readers engrossed and enthusiastic. She plans the beginnings of her books and, even if she is not sure exactly what will happen by the end, she knows the kind of things that are likely to happen.

Characters

It is through these dramatic plots that her characters are revealed. It is how they react to different situations that tells you what kind of people they are and how well they can cope with all the things that can happen to them. She is equally at home with boys and girls and she gives all her characters very active roles. They are mostly very busy doing things, rather than spending their lives sitting around and discussing their feelings. In *Swimathon!*, for example, Clipper, doesn't say much about not being able to swim. She certainly doesn't apologise to the others for letting them down. In fact, she thinks that they are stupid to have entered her for an event that she can't take part in. But, her constant attempts to try swimming show just how keen she is to live up to her reputation as a great sportswoman. Clipper is just one example of the kind of optimistic and hopeful characters that Gillian likes to write about. They usually seem to expect that the best will happen, rather than dreading the worst.

Whoever they are and whatever their situation in life they have to find their own resources to draw on. In *Twin and Super-Twin,* Midge, David and Ben have to think quickly when they attack the Albert Street bonfire, and they have to be brave to stand up to the bullying from the rival gang. Like many of Gillian's other charac-

Swimathon!

Twin and Super-Twin

ters they have to use a combination of brains and strength to extract themselves from the situations they get into. For older readers of books such as *A Map of Nowhere* and *Pictures in the Dark* the situations are a lot more dangerous and the characters need a particular kind of courage and self-knowledge to get through. But they, too, have to rely on their own resources to find a way out. There is no fudging of the realities by providing an easy answer.

A Map of Nowhere

Pictures in the Dark

Super-human powers: *The Demon Headmaster*

The Demon Headmaster series

The obvious exceptions to the stories which revolve around convincingly real characters and events are those books of Gillian's which move beyond what is possible in reality. The idea of giving a character super-human powers adds an extra dimension to these stories and allows her a freer hand to invent both the situations and the way in which characters respond to them. She used it first in *The Demon Headmaster*, which was only her seventh book. The idea had actually come to her in a story that was being told in an earlier book, *Save Our School*. One of her own children pointed out what an interesting story it was and Gillian, too, was excited by its possibilities. And so was born what is now Gillian's most famous book, series of books and TV series.

Lloyd and Harvey, together with the other members of SPLAT, need all the help they can get to resist the powers of their terrible headmaster. All the other pupils, and especially the prefects, are under his hypnotic spell. When Dinah comes to live with them she finds that she, too, can resist and she joins SPLAT as it works to break the headmaster's control. Gillian's descriptions of the schools and the way that the pupils behave seem all too familiar, which makes the idea of the hypnotic head particularly convincing – and frightening. The use of his super-human powers is really chilling and adds an interesting twist to a traditional school story. SPLAT have to use a little bit more skill than usual to defeat the Demon Headmaster and even so, as the many sequels show, he has a horrible trick of coming back again.

Research

For all her books, and especially her historical novels such as *The Great Elephant Chase*, Gillian has to do a great deal of research. She is careful to make sure that all the details are accurate but never falls into the trap of writing something that sounds like a text book or catalogue of information. She brings the world she describes vividly to life through her characters' responses to their situations. In two recent books, *Chartbreak*, set in the pop world, and *New World*, which takes a scary look at what might happen when virtual reality becomes all too real, she applies the same research principles to contemporary situations so that all the spe-

The Great Elephant Chase

Chartbreak

New World

cific and technical facts are accurate. This means that the backgrounds are perfectly drawn so that all the action seems quite convincing.

Whether in the past or the present, Gillian Cross writes a lot about social conflict and the way in which some people get a raw deal out of life. She believes strongly that everyone should have a fair chance and that in all situations the weak should protect the strong. Sometimes she chooses public causes as in *Save our School* or *Revolt at Ratcliffe's Rags*. At other times she writes about the freedom of individuals to find themselves and their own identity. Because her characters have courage and boldness, they are able to stand up for what they believe in. And fight. She comes out strongly against bullies, whether they are children bullying other children or adults repressing children, and she often shows how powerful children can be when they are working together.

Gillian's books are excellent adventure sto-

Save Our School

Revolt at Ratcliffe's Rags

ries that are exciting to read and very satisfying when you have finished them. They are made memorable by her sparky characters and her strong sense of fair play. She knows children and she likes them. That's why she's such a good children's book writer.

Julia Eccleshare
1999

Bibliography
In date order

The Runaway

illustrated by Reginald Gray
Methuen 1979 (Magnet paperback)

Rather than face life in a council home, Denny runs away. He meets up with Nachtar and begins the adventure of surviving without being discovered by the grown-ups.

The Iron Way

illustrated by Tony Morris

Oxford University Press 1979

A story about the struggles and conflicts in a 19th-century Sussex village when the navvies arrive to build the railway.

Revolt at Ratcliffe's Rags

illustrated by Tony Morris

Oxford University Press 1980 (published in Magnet paperback as *Strike at Ratcliffe's Rags*)

When Abby and her friends choose a local clothing factory as the subject for their project, they get caught up in a struggle for justice.

*The Barny, Spag and Clipper series**

Stories about three friends and their crazy adventures in and around Bennett School.

Save Our School*

illustrated by Gareth Floyd

Methuen 1981 (Mammoth paperback)

The Mintyglo Kid*

illustrated by Gareth Floyd

Methuen 1983 (Mammoth paperback)

Swimathon!*

illustrated by Gareth Floyd

Methuen 1986 (Mammoth paperback)

Gobbo the Great*

illustrated by Philippe Dupasquier

Methuen 1991 (Mammoth paperback)

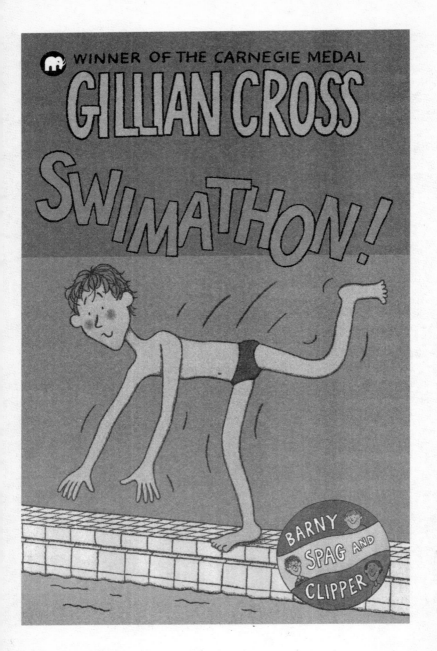

GILLIAN CROSS

GOBBO THE GREAT

BARNY
SPAG AND
CLIPPER

A Whisper of Lace

Oxford University Press 1981

What is inside the coffin that is brought over from France?
A story of lace-smuggling in the 18th century.

*The Demon Headmaster series**

Lloyd and Harvey, together with the other members of
SPLAT, need all the help they can get to resist the hypnotic
powers of their terrible headmaster.

The Demon Headmaster*

illustrated by Gary Rees
Oxford University Press 1982 (Puffin paperback)

The Prime Minister's Brain*

illustrated by Sally Burgess
Oxford University Press 1985 (Puffin paperback)

The Revenge of the Demon Headmaster*
(originally published as: *Hunky Parker is Watching You*)
illustrated by Maureen Bradley

Oxford University Press 1994 (Puffin paperback)

The Demon Headmaster Strikes Again*

illustrated by Maureen Bradley

Oxford University Press 1996 (Puffin paperback)

The Demon Headmaster Takes Over*

illustrated by Maureen Bradley

Oxford University Press 1997 (Puffin paperback)

The Dark Behind the Curtain

illustrated by David Parkins

Oxford University Press 1982 (Hippo paperback)

A school production of *Sweeney Todd* summons up ghostly frightened children from Victorian times.

Born of the Sun

illustrated by Mark Edwards

Oxford University Press 1983 (Mammoth paperback)

When Paula goes on a trip to South America with her parents to find the lost city of Atahualpa she thinks it will be the journey of a lifetime – until her father's erratic behaviour leads her to question the real reasons for the trip they're making.

On the Edge

Oxford University Press 1984 (Puffin paperback)

Can Tug, the son of a famous journalist, survive the physical and mental pressure of being a hostage?

Chartbreak

Oxford University Press 1986 (Puffin paperback)

Janis runs away from home to join a rock band and her whole life changes for ever.

Roscoe's Leap

Oxford University Press 1987 (Puffin paperback)

To Hannah, living in a weird and fantastical old house means constantly having to fix things like the central heating. To Stephen, it is a place where something terrifying once happened to him – something he doesn't want to remember, but can't quite forget.

A Map of Nowhere

Oxford University Press 1988 (Mammoth paperback)

Nick's older brother has given him an undercover quest which raises uncomfortable questions and Nick has to

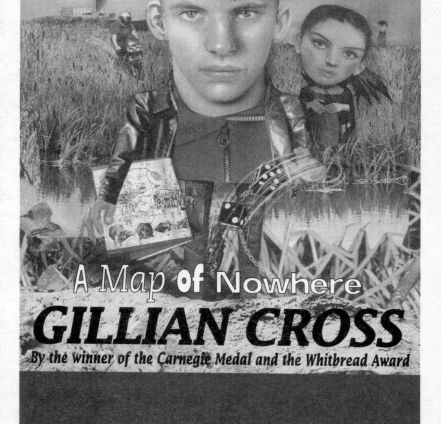

A Map **of** Nowhere

GILLIAN CROSS

By the winner of the Carnegie Medal and the Whitbread Award

decide not only where his loyalties lie, but also what sort of person he wants to be.

Rescuing Gloria

illustrated by Gareth Floyd
Methuen 1989 (Mammoth paperback)

Rescuing the goat is only the start of Leo's problems. Soon he and his friends have a whole menagerie of ducks, hens and other strays to look after – without the adults finding out.

The Monster from Underground

illustrated by Peter Firmin
Heinemann 1990

Bomber hates writing. So he isn't pleased when his teacher tells him to keep a Nature Diary – especially when bossy Harriet from next door makes fun of his ideas. But then he finds some peculiar objects in Harriet's garden and very strange things begin to happen.

Twin and Super-Twin

illustrated by Maureen Bradley
Oxford University Press 1990 (Puffin paperback)

Midge, David and Ben have to think quickly when they attack the Albert Street bonfire, and be brave to stand up to the bullying of the rival gang.

Wolf
Oxford University Press 1990 (Puffin paperback)

Cassy hears sinister footsteps in the middle of the night. Suddenly she is packed off to stay with her beautiful and feckless mother. There is no explanation. Something has gone frighteningly wrong.

Winner of the Carnegie Medal 1990

Rent-A-Genius
illustrated by Glenys Ambrus
Hamish Hamilton 1991 (Puffin paperback)

Sophy always knows best and her family is sick of it. 'Find someone who really needs your help,' says her mother. So Sophy sets up Rent-A-Genius and the problems come flocking in.

The Great Elephant Chase
Oxford University Press 1992 (Puffin paperback)

Penniless and parentless, Tad and Cissie decide to make

their way across America to a better life – not an easy feat when you're trying to hide an enormous elephant.

Winner of the Smarties Prize 1992
Winner of the Whitbread Children's Novel Award 1992

The Furry Maccaloo
illustrated by Madeleine Baker
Heinemann, 1993

A strange furry animal appears at school and demands all kinds of impossible things from Surinder. She and her friend David have to work hard to keep the 'Maccaloo' happy. But will they ever find a way to get it back to the Delta-world where it belongs?

Beware Olga!
illustrated by Arthur Robins
Walker 1993

Fiona hates the outside of things – skin, peel, crusts – and refuses to eat any of them. So when Olga come to tea, Fiona is delighted. For Olga loves eating outsides. The only trouble is she doesn't know when to stop!

The Tree House

illustrated by Paul Howard

Methuen 1993 (Mammoth Paperback)

Sprog and William long to have a tree house, but their father has to go abroad before it can be completed. Will the tree house ever be finished?

What Will Emily Do?

illustrated by Paul Howard

Methuen 1994 (Mammoth Paperback)

Matthew can't wait to start school – until he realises he won't know what his younger sister Emily is up to!

Illustration by Nick Sharratt for *The Crazy Shoe Shuffle*

New World

Oxford University Press 1994 (Puffin paperback)

A scary look at what might happen when virtual reality becomes all too real.

The Crazy Shoe Shuffle

illustrated by Nick Sharratt

Methuen 1995

Three of the teachers at Lee's school find themselves in the children's shoes – and they're right out of step with everyone else!

Posh Watson

illustrated by Mike Gordon

Walker 1995

Have you ever thought of wearing trumpet trainers? Whatever Posh Watson wears sets a new fashion. Can the school ever keep up?

The Roman Beanfeast

illustrated by Linzi Henry

Hamish Hamilton 1996 (Puffin paperback)

Davey's class is doing a project on the Romans. Davey is determined to win the prize that will be awarded at the Roman feast at the end of term, but so is Molly – and she'll do anything to beat him.

Pictures in the Dark

Oxford University Press 1996 (Puffin paperback)

When Charlie photographs an unknown creature swimming in the river one night, he has little idea of the effect it will have on his life, or the weird events that will be set in motion.

The Goose Girl

illustrated by Jason Cockcroft

Scholastic 1998

Once upon a time there was a princess who lost everything she had . . . A retelling of the well-known story collected by the Brothers Grimm.

Tightrope

Oxford University Press 1999

It was the best wall in the world and there was nothing on

it at all. Not a mark. It was just waiting for Ashley to get up there and tag it. But she didn't know that someone would be watching her, stalking her.